Our World

DESERTS

Keith Lye

Silver Burdett Press
Morristown, New Jersey

Titles in this series

Deserts

Polar Regions

Jungles and Rainforests

Rivers and Lakes

Mountains

Seas and Oceans

First published in 1987 by
Wayland (Publishers) Ltd
61 Western Road, Hove
East Sussex BN3 1JD. England

Adapted and first published in the
United States in 1987 by
Silver Burdett Press
Morristown, New Jersey

Edited by Andrew Kelly

U.S. edition edited by Joanne Fink

Designed by Malcolm Smythe

Typeset by DP Press. Sevenoaks, Kent
Printed in Italy by G. Canale & C.S.p.A., Turin

Front cover, main picture Sand dunes in Death Valley
National Monument, California.
Front cover, inset Frilled lizard in threat display,
Australia.
Back cover Camel postman, Bikaner, India.

Library of Congress Cataloging-in-Publication Data

Lye, Keith.
    Deserts.
    (Our world)
    Bibliography: p.
    Includes index.
    Summary: Describes the characteristics of
different kinds of deserts and the plants, animals,
and people that make their home in them.
    1. Deserts—Juvenile literature.   [1. Deserts]
I. Title.   II. Series.
GB611.L93   1987   910'.0915'4   87–12680
ISBN 0–382–09501–4

Contents

Hot and cold deserts

A desert is usually thought of as a hot, dry place. Not all deserts are hot. Some deserts are cold for much of the year, and even in deserts that are very hot during the day, temperatures can drop to below freezing at night. But all deserts are dry. There is very little precipitation in a desert – precipitation means all forms of water that come from the air including rain, sleet, snow, hail, frost, mist, and dew. The average precipitation in deserts is generally less than 4 in (100 mm) a year. But places with 20 in (500 mm) of rain a year can also be arid (dry) and barren if temperatures and evaporation rates are high. In fact, experts estimate that one-third of the world's land is arid to some extent. Arid land has very little vegetation.

Hot deserts, including the Sahara, lie in subtropical zones. The Sahara is the largest of the world's deserts. Its area is 3,250,000 sq miles (8,400,000 sq km), which makes it larger than the continent of Australia. Some hot deserts are along coasts, for example the Namib Desert in southern Africa. Cold deserts lie far from the sea in the higher latitudes – between the subtropical hot deserts and the polar regions. High latitude cold deserts include the Gobi Desert of Central Asia and the Patagonian Desert of South America.

The Arctic lands and Antarctica are also kinds of deserts, because the cold air over them is extremely dry. For example, near the South Pole, the average precipitation is only 4–6 in (100–150 mm) a year. But these icy regions differ in so many ways from the hot and cold deserts mentioned above that this book does not deal with them.

Hot and cold deserts are hostile places. They are thinly populated, but even the harshest deserts contain specially adapted plants, animals, and people.

Most people think of deserts as being covered in sand but some deserts are covered in gravel and boulders while in others the bedrock has been exposed.

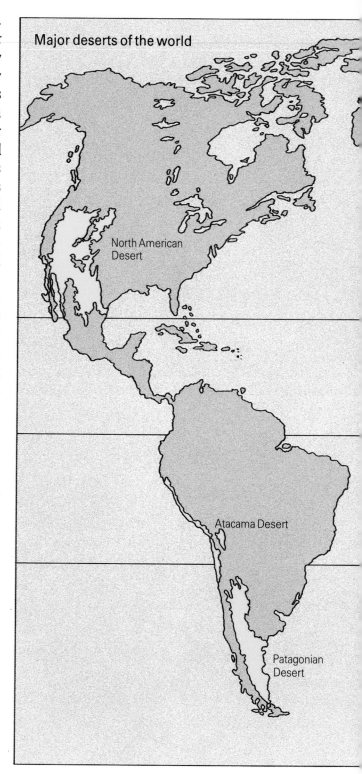

Major deserts of the world

North American Desert

Atacama Desert

Patagonian Desert

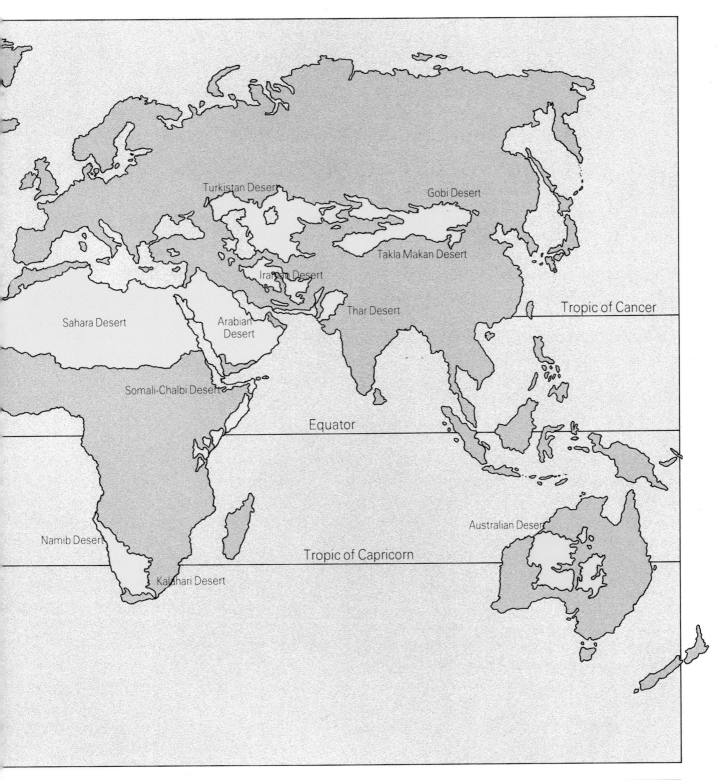

Turkistan Desert

Gobi Desert

Takla Makan Desert

Iranian Desert

Sahara Desert

Arabian Desert

Thar Desert

Tropic of Cancer

Somali-Chalbi Desert

Equator

Namib Desert

Australian Desert

Tropic of Capricorn

Kalahari Desert

Water in deserts

Desert travelers have died of thirst when water was only 328 ft (100 m) away – under their feet – in rock layers called aquifers. Some aquifers contain water that seeped down from the surface thousands of years ago when the desert had a moist climate. Others contain water that fell on mountains thousands of miles away, where the aquifers are exposed. Some aquifers are made of porous sandstone, which contains tiny pores (spaces) through which water flows. Other aquifers are made of solid rock, such as limestone, but water seeps through networks of cracks in them. All aquifers are permeable, which means that the cracks or pores are connected so that the water can flow through the rock.

Ground water emerges on the surface at oases, many of which are fertile, densely populated places. Some are in deep basins, where water flows onto the land from an exposed aquifer. Other oases are

These Tuaregs are filling their water bags at a well in Niger in the southern Sahara.

Oases

Oases form where water from an aquifer comes to the surface. An aquifer is a layer of rock through which water can flow. Such material is permeable, that is it has many tiny spaces that are connected. This enables the water to flow through it. The aquifer is often sandwiched between layers of impermeable rock, that is rock through which water cannot flow. The water in the aquifer is usually under pressure so that when there is a break in the overlying rock the water rises to the surface. This break may be due to a well being dug, or to a basin being eroded till the aquifer is exposed, or to a fault – a break and shift in the rock layers which is due to stress in the Earth's crust.

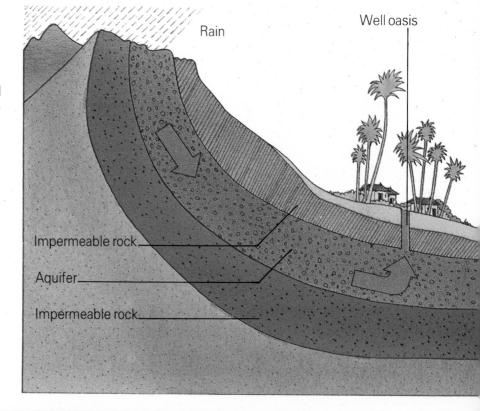

Rain

Well oasis

Impermeable rock

Aquifer

Impermeable rock

This is a river valley oasis called Tinerhir on the edge of the Sahara in Morocco.

found where movements along faults (breaks) in the rocks block the flow of water through an aquifer (see diagram below). The water is then forced to rise to the surface along the fault.

Some oases are around wells, which have been dug down to aquifers. But the largest oases are river valleys, including the Nile Valley in the eastern Sahara. The Nile's headstreams rise in the well-watered highlands of East Africa and the river flows through Sudan and Egypt to the Mediterranean Sea. The bulk of the population of these countries lives on its banks.

Oases have been important in history. For instance, the valleys of the Nile, the Indus River in Pakistan, and the Euphrates and Tigris Rivers in Iraq were all sites of great civilizations in deserts.

However, not all water from aquifers is suitable for farming. Some is too salty and will kill most plants.

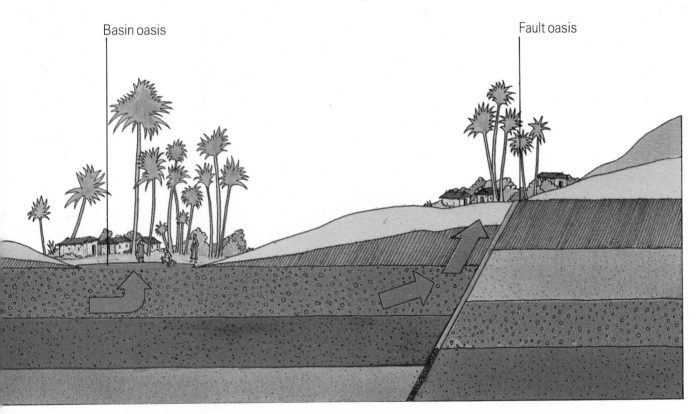

Basin oasis

Fault oasis

Water erosion

Many land features in deserts were shaped by running water. Some were formed long ago, when the regions had much more rain. For instance, the Sahara was a grassland with many streams only 10,000 years ago and cave paintings show the many animals that lived there. But 5,000 years later, the Sahara had become a desert.

Water also helps to shape the land today, when rare, heavy downpours cause floods. The flood water picks up loose rock, ranging from dust to large boulders, and sweeps them along valleys, deepening and broadening them as it surges along. These normally dry valleys are called wadis in North Africa and Arabia and arroyos in the Americas. Such floods have drowned people foolish enough to camp in wadis. The water dumps the loose rocks on the beds of temporary lakes, called playas, or at the foot of slopes. At the bottom of some slopes, loose rock piles up in heaps, called

Here in Death Valley a series of alluvial fans, made during desert storms, forms a bajada.

Canyons, mesas, and buttes

In deserts where the rocks are in horizontal layers, some of which are hard and others of which are soft, distinctive landforms develop. Where there has been little erosion there is a plateau, although the plateau may have deep canyons cut in it by rivers. The face of the plateau is eroded away leaving flat-topped "islands" of rock. The large islands are called mesas. As time passes and erosion does its work, the mesa becomes smaller and smaller until a small, steep-sided peak called a butte is left. In time the butte, too, is eroded away. Where there is a hard layer these landforms have a cliff with a steep face and where there is a soft layer they have a sloping face.

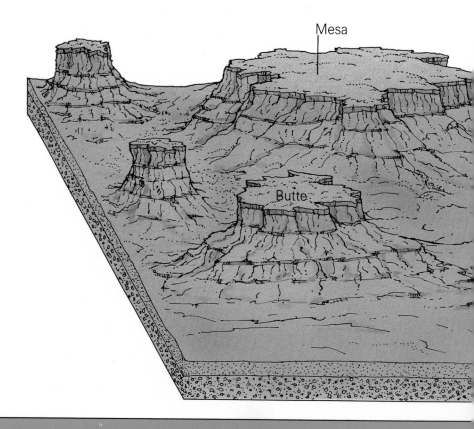

alluvial fans or cones. Aprons of loose rock formed when several alluvial fans merge together are called bajadas (or bahadas).

Canyons are also desert features that have been formed by water. A canyon is a narrow, deep, steep-sided gorge or valley. It is formed by a river cutting down through soft rocks in an arid region. Because there is little rain, the rate of weathering of the canyon walls is very slow, so the walls are steep. In wetter climates rain erodes the sides of the valley, especially the tops, so the sides slope and form a broad "V."

Water erosion has created badland areas in many arid regions. Badlands consist of complex networks of deep valleys. Other desert features, such as mesas (flat-topped mountains) and buttes (jagged columns of rock), were made by running water, though they are also the result of the work of another natural force – wind erosion.

These badlands in the Iranian desert show the many heavily eroded gulleys typical of badlands.

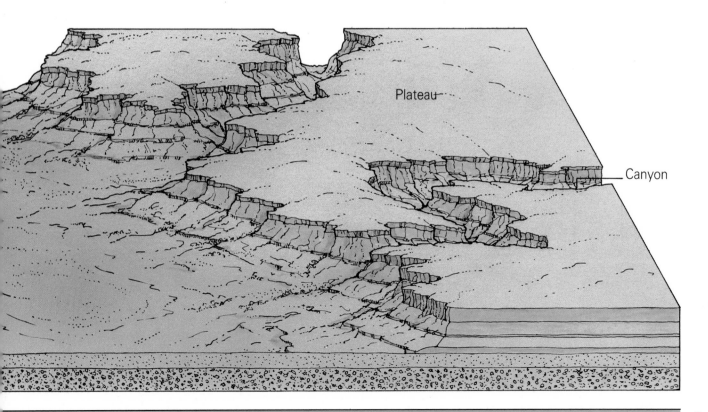

Plateau

Canyon

Wind erosion

Besides heat and aridity, deserts have another notable climatic feature – powerful winds that cause unpleasant duststorms and sandstorms. Winds lift dust 9,500 ft (3,000 m) or more into the air and carry it long distances. For example, in Australia, raindrops are sometimes turned red by dust blown from faraway deserts.

Winds lift medium-sized sand grains up to about 5 ft (1.5 m) into the air. These grains move forward by bouncing across the ground – a process called saltation. Large grains, too heavy to be lifted, are rolled across the surface.

Sand consists mainly of grains of the hard mineral quartz. Wind-blown sand acts like an abrasive, whose effect is similar to that of sand-blasters used to clean dirty city buildings. In severe sandstorms, wind-blown sand can strip the paint from cars and pit windshields so that one cannot see through them.

Wind-blown sand is one of the main forms of erosion in deserts. Because sand is usually not lifted very high in the air by the wind, erosion occurs mostly on the lower parts of the rocks and boulders. It wears out small caves in the bottoms of cliffs, etches soft rock layers, cuts lines of weakness into deep grooves, and undercuts rocks to form fantastic features called zeugen. These include rock pillars, mushroom rocks (which consist of large boulders perched on narrow stems), natural arches, and yardangs. Yardangs are steep-sided, overhanging ridges ranging in length from a few inches to half a mile. Pebbles on the ground are often carved into shapes resembling brazil nuts, while the sand grains themselves are gradually rounded. Sand composed of rounded grains is often called millet-seed sand.

Wind-blown sand also causes deflation – the wearing of depressions in the desert's surface. Wind first blows away loose dust and sand grains to create a hollow and when rock is exposed it is worn away. Eventually, however, basins are worn down to an aquifer. Wind erosion then ceases, because water binds loose sand grains together. The largest wind-carved basin in the world is the Qattara Depression in Egypt. It is about the size of Massachusetts.

Saltation

In a sandstorm the wind bounces the sand grains along the surface of the desert in a process called saltation. A grain of sand is lifted into the air by the wind and when it drops back to earth the impact bounces it back into the air. Such grains erode overhangs in boulders and rockfaces.

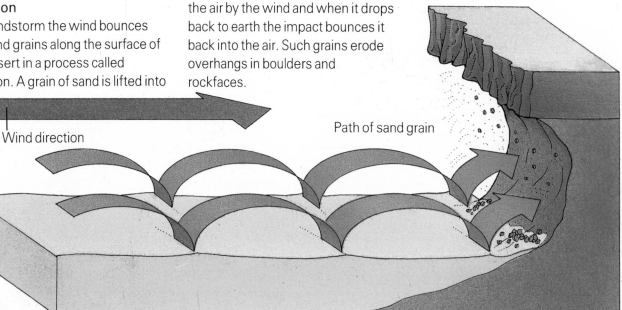

Wind direction

Path of sand grain

Left This zeugen, a rock undercut by wind-blown sand to form a fantastic shape, is in Algeria.

Below These rocks in the Sahara have been rounded and smoothed by wind-blown sand.

Land features in deserts

Sand covers about one-fifth of the world's deserts. Sandy deserts, which are among the world's most hostile places, are known by their Arabic name, erg. Stony desert is called reg (or gibber plains in Australia), while bare rocky landscapes are called hammada.

Large flat areas that are filled by shallow lakes after heavy rains are called playas or chotts. They are ideal for auto racing. Some, such as Lake Eyre in Australia, have been used for attempts on world land speed records. Some playas are covered by salt. The Danakil Depression in north-eastern Ethiopia has salt deposits that are more than 3 miles (5 km) thick in places. Once part of the Red Sea, this depression was isolated by lava flows. The salt was left behind as the seawater evaporated.

Sandy deserts contain varied land features, including many types of dunes. Dunes are like waves in the sand; they reflect the patterns of the winds. If the winds are variable, the sand may pile

These dunes are at Eucla in Western Australia. Dunes are constantly moving and changing shape.

Dunes

Dunes form where the wind has piled sand up into ridges or mounds. They often take definite shapes. Where the wind blows mainly from one direction longitudinal dunes form. These are dunes whose ridges run in the same direction as the wind. A seif dune forms when a wind sometimes blows at right angles to the prevailing wind. This means the ridges, instead of being straight as in longitudinal dunes, wander back and forth. Barchan dunes form when a prevailing wind piles up sand around an obstacle, such as a boulder. They are crescent shaped with a gently sloping windward side and a steeper leeward side.

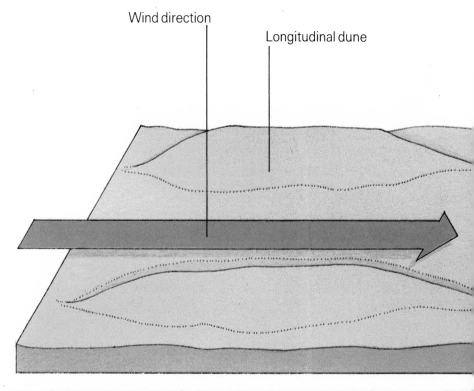

Wind direction

Longitudinal dune

This playa is in Tunisia. Notice the tire tracks in the firm layer of salt on the surface.

up in shapeless mounds, though star-shaped dunes are sometimes formed. When there is a prevailing (dominant) wind, the sand often piles up into longitudinal ridges parallel to the wind direction. Seif dunes (seif is Arabic for sword) are sinuous, knife-edged, longitudinal dunes. They appear when a second wind blows occasionally at right angles to the prevailing wind.

The best known dunes are crescent-shaped barchans, which often form when sand piles up against an obstacle, such as a boulder. The wind blows sand up the gently sloping windward side of barchans and down the steep leeward side. Desert travelers sometimes hear strange roaring sounds, caused by large amounts of sand slumping down the steep slope.

Dunes are always moving. A dune in the Soviet Union once advanced by 66 ft (20 m) in a single day. But the usual rate of advance is 20–30 ft (6–9 m) a year. Whole cities have been buried by dunes.

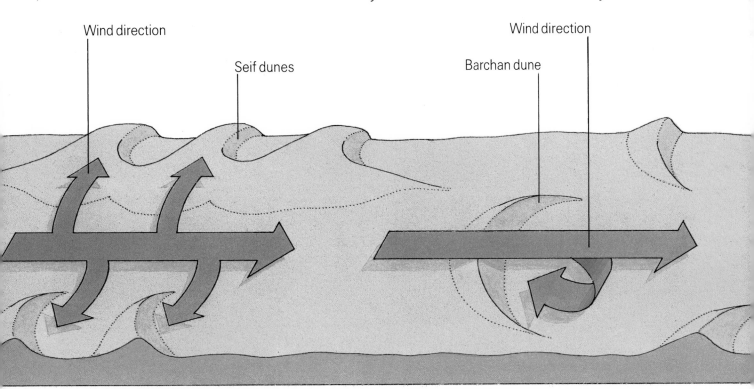

Wind direction

Seif dunes

Wind direction

Barchan dune

Subtropical deserts

Subtropical hot deserts extend around the world in two zones. These zones, called the horse latitudes, lie on either side of latitudes 30° north and 30° south (see diagram below). In the Northern Hemisphere, they include the enormous Sahara, the Arabian and Iranian Deserts, the Indo-Pakistani Thar Desert, and the Sonoran Desert in the Americas. In the Southern Hemisphere, they include the Atacama Desert in South America, the Namib and Kalahari Deserts in Africa, and the massive Australian Desert (see pages 4–5).

There is not only little rain in these deserts but it is also very unreliable. Years may pass with hardly any rain, and then 3 in (75 mm) may be recorded during an hour-long, freak storm.

These deserts also hold the record for high temperatures. The highest air temperature measured in the shade, 136.4° F (58° C), was recorded at Al-Aziziyah, Libya, in the Sahara. And the place with the highest average yearly temperature (in the shade) – 94° F (34.4° C) – is Dallol in Ethiopia's salt-encrusted Danakil Depression. Temperatures are even higher in the sun. Around midday in the Sahara, the temperature of the soil may reach 189° F (87° C). The world record for sunshine is held by the eastern Sahara,

Deserts and air circulation

Subtropical deserts are a result of the way air circulates around the earth. This circulation is powered by the sun. The sun heats the air at the equator (where the Earth is hottest). When air is heated it rises. The rising air creates a low pressure zone of little wind near the equator called the doldrums. As it rises, it cools and spreads out to the north and south. When it is cool enough it sinks back to land. This occurs around latitudes 30° south and 30° north of the equator. These zones are called the horse latitudes and are zones of high pressure. As the air sinks, it becomes warm and dry and when it reaches the Earth, it dries and warms the land creating deserts. Desert climates are not only hot and dry but also stable. The warm dry winds blow outwards, notably the trade winds that blow from the east toward the equator and the westerly winds that blow toward the Poles.

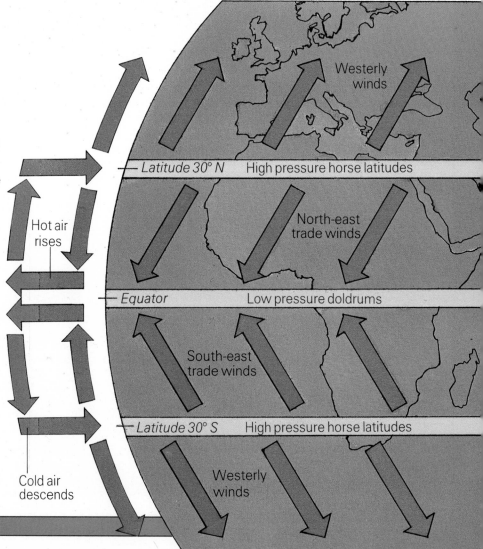

The Sonoran Desert is a subtropical desert in North America. It is noted for its many types of cactus.

which has over 4,300 hours of sunshine a year.

The lack of clouds at night has an important effect on desert climates. In many parts of the world, clouds help to keep the air warm because they reflect back much of the heat that is radiated upward from the ground. But in cloudless deserts, most of this radiated heat escapes into space. As a result, temperatures often plummet after dark, sometimes to below the freezing point. There may be as much as 81° F (45° C) difference in temperature between day and night, which partly explains why many desert nomads wear thick clothes.

The Olgas are a range of hills in the subtropical Australian Desert. Few plants grow there.

Coastal and inland deserts

Two subtropical deserts are on coasts – namely the Atacama Desert in South America and the Namib Desert in southwestern Africa. These deserts are cooler and more humid than other subtropical deserts, but they are extremely arid. The cooling is caused by cold offshore currents: the Humboldt (or Peru) current off western South America and the Benguela current off southwestern Africa. Both currents contain cold water from the seas around Antarctica. Winds blowing over these currents are chilled and they lose much of their moisture over the sea. The remaining moisture, instead of forming rain clouds, forms mist and fog. For example, the port of Swakopmund in Namibia has an average annual precipitation of .5 in (12 mm), mostly in the form of mist. Farther inland, the air becomes warmer and drier, creating extremely bleak desert conditions.

Cold deserts lie in the high latitudes, north and south of the subtropical deserts. Some are in rain shadow regions, on the leeward sides of mountains. Rain shadow regions occur when moist winds from the sea lose most of the moisture as they ascend a mountain range. As air rises it expands and cools and its moisture condenses to fall as rain or snow. Beyond the crest, they descend, become warmer, and pick up moisture. High latitude rain shadow deserts include the Great Basin in the western United States and the Patagonia Desert, east of the Andes, South America.

Other high latitude deserts lie far beyond the reach of moist, oceanic winds. The biggest is the Gobi Desert, in central Asia, where, in summer, air temperatures in the shade reach 115° F (46° C). The average precipitation is less than 10 in (250 mm) a year and some falls as snow.

High latitude cold deserts include the Ustyurt Plateau, the Kara Kum Desert, and the Kyzyl Kum Desert east of the Caspian Sea in the Soviet Union. Another cold desert in southwestern China is named Takla Makan, a term meaning "the place from which there is no return."

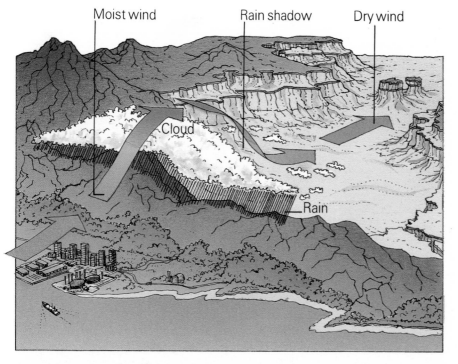

Moist wind   Rain shadow   Dry wind

Cloud

Rain

Left Many inland deserts lie in rain shadows. Rain shadows occur where there is a mountain range in the path of moist winds. The mountain range forces the air to rise, and as the air rises it cools. Cool air cannot hold as much moisture as warm air so clouds form and then release moisture as rain, snow, or hail. When the wind blows down the other side, it is very dry. It contains no moisture to fall as rain and it picks up moisture from the land.

Right The Namib Desert is a coastal desert in southern Africa.

Desert plants

To survive in deserts, plants must withstand long droughts and high temperatures. Yet plants grow in most deserts, though they are widely scattered.

Many small desert plants, called ephemerals, produce seeds that lie dormant for years, but after a rainstorm, they complete their life cycle in six to eight weeks. For example, the chief plants in Australia's Simpson Desert are normally hardy shrubs and spinifex grass. But after rain, millions of flowering ephemerals spring to life, producing a scene of great beauty and food for insects, birds, and other animals. But the plants are soon gone. Only their seeds remain.

Some plants are drought-tolerant. For example, the creosote bush in North America can survive a year without water. Some plants, such as the ocotillo (or coach whip), shed their leaves during droughts and regrow them after rain. Other plants, called succulents, are very fleshy and are capable of storing large amounts of water. These include the cacti of the Americas and euphorbias in the Old World. The saguaro, the largest cactus, often reaches 50 ft (15 m) in height. It has an extensive root system and stores 6–8 tons of water in its trunk and branches, while the smaller barrel cactus has often provided water for thirsty travelers. The African aloe also stores water in its stem, while such succulents as yuccas and agaves store water in their leaves. Succulents often have waxy surfaces to reduce water loss, or hairs to reflect sunlight and

"Drought resisters"

All desert plants face the same problem – drought. They solve it in two ways. The "drought evaders" or ephemerals appear only when there is rain; the rest of the time they lie dormant as hardy seeds. They are shown in the photograph opposite.

Examples of the other group, the "drought resisters" are shown in the illustration on this page. The drought resisters have developed many different features that enable them to avoid drying out. The saguaro cactus only grows very slowly and can store large amounts of water. It also has a root system that spreads widely just under the surface. The roots of the mesquite go down very deeply and are often thicker than its branches. It makes use of underground sources of water. The cereus stores water in underground bulbs.

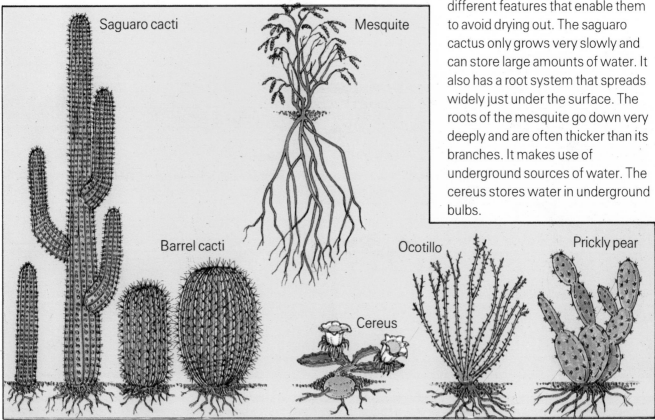

Saguaro cacti   Mesquite

Barrel cacti

Cereus

Ocotillo   Prickly pear

act as insulation. Others close their stomata (leaf pores) during the day. Some have sharp spines or an unpleasant taste to discourage animals from eating them and using their stores of water.

A few desert plants store water in bulbous roots. Others have very deep root systems. The roots of the mesquite bush often extend down for 165 ft (50 m). One of the strangest plants, the welwitschia, gets water from droplets of fog on its two large, leathery leaves. Botanists estimate that some of these ungainly plants with their wind-shredded leaves are 2,000 years old.

Left The welwitschia plant grows in the arid regions of Namibia. Its leaves can gather moisture from fog.

Below These ephemeral plants have burst into bloom after seasonal desert rains.

Desert insects, reptiles, and amphibians

Animals respond to desert conditions in many ways. In the Namib Desert, a black beetle stands on its head on the crest of sand dunes. Droplets of water carried on the wind are caught on its body and trickle down into its open mouth.

Arthropods, including insects, spiders, and scorpions, are abundant in deserts. Most spend the hottest parts of the day in rocky crevices or underground. The famous desert locust needs water and plenty of plants for food and shelter. Large populations occur only after rains, when ephemeral plants are abundant. As the plants die off, the locusts are confined to smaller areas. Eventually, they launch themselves into the air in huge swarms.

Many species of ants live in deep nests. The honey ants of the Sonoran Desert store moisture by filling worker ants with nectar and other liquids. These ants swell up like grapes and hang from the roof of the nest until their liquid is needed. Similar ants are found in the Australian Desert. The Australian Aborigines dig them up and eat them as a sweet delicacy.

Desert reptiles include snakes and lizards. As carnivores, snakes get liquid from their food and they reduce moisture loss by spending the daylight hours in cool burrows. Lizards are much more common than snakes. Some have transparent eyelids to protect their eyes. Others have scales or webbing on their feet to help them walk across sand.

Among the few desert amphibians are toads, which aestivate (this means hibernate but during dry, not cold, periods) by burying themselves. The spadefoot toad in the Sonoran Desert lives underground until it is alerted by vibrations caused by heavy raindrops. It then emerges, mates, and lays eggs in pools. As the puddles dry up, the tadpoles have to struggle to survive. They must be mature enough to be able to aestivate before the rainwater disappears or they will die.

Sidewinder snakes have developed a sideways method of movement that minimizes contact with the hot sand. The snake lifts first the front part of the body and then the rear part of the body, leaving a series of parallel tracks.

When the dune lizard stops running on hot desert sand, it lifts its feet alternately until the sand in the shadow of its body has cooled. It then rests on its belly with four feet and its tail in the air.

This beetle (*Stenocara phalangium*), which lives in the Namib Desert, has the longest legs of any beetle.

Desert birds and mammals

Most birds in deserts must visit oases regularly to drink. The sandgrouse of Africa and Asia soaks its breast feathers in water before returning to its nest. There it moistens its eggs to keep them from overheating, or, if the eggs have hatched, its young suck the water from its feathers. Most nests are built in the shade. Only one bird, the flightless ostrich, has eggs large enough to withstand overheating. Most birds feed on insects and seeds. A few, including the American roadrunner (a type of cuckoo) and the African secretary bird, are meat-eaters. Both of them prefer to run rather than fly.

Several mammals, including kangaroo rats in North America, jerboas in the Old World, and kangaroos in Australia, also move on two feet, giving them the mobility to evade predators. Most small mammals, including kangaroo rats and jerboas, spend much of the day in cool burrows. Kangaroo rats conserve water in other ways. They

This Gila woodpecker is feeding on the red pulpy fruit of the saguaro cactus.

Red kangaroos are grazing animals that live in the deserts and grasslands of central Australia.

The jack rabbit, which is really a hare, can survive in the deserts of North America.

neither pant nor sweat and their urine, like that of many desert mammals, is highly concentrated to reduce water loss.

Domesticated animals include hairy yaks in the Gobi Desert and camels. The one-humped dromedary of North Africa and southwestern Asia, can go five to twelve days without water, depending on how hot it is and how dry the air is. The hairy two-humped Bactrian camel of central Asia is also domesticated. People once thought that camels' humps contained water. In fact, they are made of fat to provide energy when food is scarce.

Other large desert mammals include the Arabian oryx (which has been almost hunted to extinction in the wild), gazelles, and various wild asses, which also go long periods without water. Australia's deserts contain marsupials, including kangaroos and wallabies, besides some camels – the descendants of animals taken there by explorers.

Springboks used to be common over most of southern Africa but are now found mainly in the Kalahari Desert.

Survival in deserts

Though it may look hard to outsiders, life for many desert peoples is pleasant. This is because they have learned since childhood how to cope with desert conditions. Outsiders, however, face many dangers. Lack of water can kill in a short time. Starvation takes longer to kill, but is another hazard to the unwary. The effects of heat and sunburn must be avoided and such protective clothes as Arab headdresses must be worn. Care must also be taken to protect the eyes during sandstorms and duststorms. Deserts also contain insect pests. Flies spread an eye disease, trachoma, and mosquitoes spread malaria.

It is easy to get lost in deserts, as much of the interior of deserts looks the same and it can, therefore, be difficult to maintain a sense of direction. The heat of the desert can produce mirages which may lead people astray by making them believe that they can see something, for example a water hole, that isn't there.

Traveling in deserts, even in a four-wheel drive, can be dangerous. Vehicles can become stuck in the sand.

The Tuareg, a nomadic group of the Sahara, have adapted so that they can survive in the desert.

The Burke and Wills expedition was the first to cross the Australian continent from south to north. It left Melbourne in August 1860 with eighteen men and included camels specially imported from India. To reach the Gulf of Carpentaria on the north coast of Australia the expedition had to cross the deserts of central Australia. The final party of four men reached the coastal swamps in February 1861. Only one of the four survived the return journey. Both Burke and Wills died. John King, the survivor, was found living with the aborigines. It was their knowledge of desert conditions that enabled him to survive when all the elaborate preparations of the European explorers had failed.

Far right A contemporary newspaper illustration of the death of Burke.

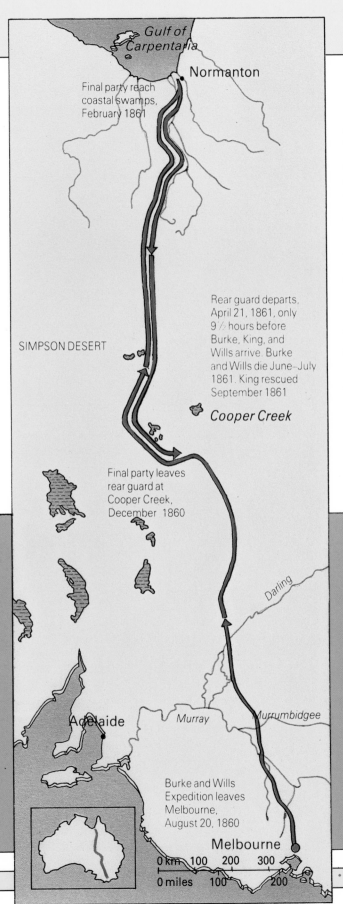

Gulf of
Carpentaria

Normanton

Final party reach
coastal swamps,
February 1861

SIMPSON DESERT

Rear guard departs,
April 21, 1861, only
9½ hours before
Burke, King, and
Wills arrive. Burke
and Wills die June–July
1861. King rescued
September 1861

Cooper Creek

Final party leaves
rear guard at
Cooper Creek,
December 1860

Darling

Adelaide   Murray   Murrumbidgee

Burke and Wills
Expedition leaves
Melbourne,
August 20, 1860

Melbourne

0 km   100   200   300

0 miles   100   200

Yet deserts have attracted and still attract adventurous travelers. One, the Venetian, Marco Polo (1254–1324), traveled to China across the cold deserts of central Asia with his father and uncle while he was still in his teens. The Sahara, however, was regarded by Europeans as a barrier to the inland exploration of Africa until the nineteenth century. But Arab caravans crossed it frequently, which explains why most information about early civilizations south of the Sahara comes from Arab writings.

Camels were once the chief form of transportation in deserts. The first motorized expeditions took place in the 1920s, when the American Roy Chapman Andrews (1884–1960) explored the Gobi Desert. But cars and aircraft are now common sights, especially in mineral-rich deserts. Even by car, desert travel can be dangerous. Cars and even trucks can easily become bogged down in the sand. Desert roads, where they exist, can be very rough and cars frequently break down.

Desert hunters and gatherers

People did not obtain food by farming until about 10,000 years ago. Before then, they hunted animals and gathered wild berries, nuts, and roots. A few hunting and gathering societies still exist. Two of them, the San people (or Bushmen) of the Kalahari in southern Africa, and some groups of Australian Aborigines, live in dry lands.

Much of the Kalahari is a semi-desert, with practically no surface water for most of the year. The San people, however, know places where they can suck water from the ground through reeds. They then store this water in ostrich eggs. The men are skilled hunters, who use poison-tipped arrows. The women gather plant food, using grubbing sticks to obtain roots, tubers, and bulbs that often contain water. The San people live in bands, and move camp five or six times a year. During severe droughts, they split up into family groups and forage over large areas.

Some Australian Aborigines live by hunting and gathering and their traditional knowledge of the land and where to find water and food, according to the season, is profound. They are expert hunters, using boomerangs and spears launched by woomeras (throwing sticks). But the women, who do most of the gathering, usually make a much more reliable contribution to the food supply.

Hunting and gathering societies are well adapted to desert environments and do not harm the land as farming often does. And, the hunter-gatherers have considerable artistic ability, revealed in their cave paintings, artifacts, dances, music, body decorations, and complex religious beliefs, that are expressed in rich oral (spoken) literatures.

Inset The women of Bushmen tribes are responsible for gathering plant foods, which provide a more reliable source of food than hunting.

Right Hunting is an activity usually done by men among desert groups, such as these Australian Aborigines.

Nomadic farmers of the desert

Until recent times, many desert peoples in the Old World reared livestock and moved around in search of pasture. They were proud, independent, and sometimes war-like people, who were also famed for their hospitality.

Nomadic farmers still live in the hot deserts of North Africa and southwestern and central Asia. They include the Tuaregs of the central Sahara, the Beja in eastern Sudan, the Somalis in the Horn of Africa, and the Bedouin of southwestern Asia. These peoples use dromedary camels and donkeys as beasts of burden, and rear cattle, goats, and sheep. The Tuaregs and Bedouin are also fine horsemen, though horses are better adapted to the cold deserts of central Asia, which were once dominated by mounted Mongol warriors. The Mongols once ruled China and their armies swept to the borders of Europe in the twelfth and thirteenth centuries. Mongolian nomads also rear Bactrian camels and yaks, as well as cattle, goats, and sheep. Many nomads in hot deserts live in tents made of animal skin or goat hair, while the tents in central Asia, called ger or yurts, consist of wooden frames covered with thick felt.

As a way of life, nomadic farming is fast disappearing. For example, many Bedouin have taken well-paid jobs in the oil industry. Many own cars and now rear camels only for meat or for racing. Other nomads have been forced to settle down. Some in North Africa have lost most of their herds during severe droughts. Others have been persuaded or compelled to abandon their way of life. Generally, governments regard nomads as a nuisance, because they evade laws, cross frontiers illegally and fail to pay taxes. And yet nomadic farming is a suitable way of life in some arid areas, providing that the herds do not overgraze the limited natural vegetation.

Tuareg

The Tuareg are a group of nomadic farmers of the Sahara. The word "Tuareg" means "people of the veil" in Arabic but, unlike other Muslim groups, it is the men, not the women, who wear veils. A Tuareg male thinks it rude to show his mouth or nose to a stranger, a woman, or an older man. It is also practical to wear a veil when traveling in the desert as it helps keep the mouth from drying out and protects the face during sand-storms. The Tuareg raise camels, sheep, goats, and cattle. Their traditional dwelling is a skin or woven-wool tent.

The Baluchi are a group of nomadic farmers who live in the arid lands of Iran and western Pakistan.

Mongols

The Mongolians live in Mongolia which lies between China and the Soviet Union in central Asia. Much of Mongolia is desert or grassland, which cannot support a settled way of life, so the Mongols are nomadic. They have herds of sheep, goats, cattle, and horses with the occasional camel, ox, or yak. These animals form the basis of the Mongol economy. Milk, cheese, and butter as well as tea and some milk form the bulk of their diet. Wool, hair, and hides are used to make tent walls and clothing. They live in special tents called yurts which have felt walls.

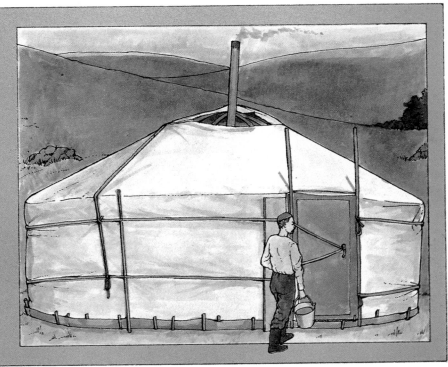

Living at oases

When the climate of a region changes, so also does the economy of its people. This happened between 10,000 and 5,000 years ago, when the Sahara was changing from a grassland into a desert. Nomadic farmers sought new lives at oases, particularly in the Nile Valley. There they found rich soil, whose fertility was renewed annually when silt was dumped by floods. They became farmers and invented simple ways of watering their fields. For example, they used a shaduf – a pole with a bucket on one end and a weight on the other – to lift water from the river. With irrigation, they grew two or three crops a year. This new way of life involved planning, the keeping of records and, above all, co-operation between people. The food surpluses led to the growth of towns and cities and the development of crafts, trade, and centralized government. Eventually, ancient Egypt, one of several great civilizations to arise in valley oases, emerged in about 3100 BC.

Many prosperous communities developed around smaller oases. Today, in North Africa and southwestern Asia, an oasis is immediately identifiable by its clusters of tall date palms. Houses are usually made of stone or sun-dried bricks. They have thick walls, often without any windows, and white walls that reflect heat. Because rain seldom comes, the roofs of most buildings are flat, providing a place where people can sleep on hot nights.

The inhabitants of oases once lived in fear of marauding nomads, who stole their possessions. That fear has gone, but natural hazards remain. The water table may fall and the oasis may dry up. The advancing sand dunes can bury oases and the surrounding fields, leaving no trace.

The Persian wheel

The Persian wheel is a device for lifting water so that fields can be irrigated. It has been used for centuries and is still in use at many oases today. A bullock is harnessed by a pole to a large wooden cog wheel. As the wheel is turned by the bullock walking in a circle, it lifts a continuous chain of buckets which have been dipped into a river or canal. As each bucket turns over at the top, it empties its water into a channel leading to a field. Donkeys or horses are sometimes used instead of a bullock. This device is called a *sakia* in Egypt and in India it is sometimes called a *harat*.

Right A Persian wheel draws up water for irrigation in India.

This is the Taghit oasis in Algeria. Notice how densely settled the area of the oasis is.

Land reclamation

Many deserts contain fertile soil, because there is no rain to wash away the chemicals that plants need. Such deserts can become rich farmland if they are watered by irrigation. Converting deserts into farmland is called land reclamation.

The Negev Desert in southern Israel has been reclaimed twice. From 200 BC, a people called the Nabataeans built step-like terraces down the hillsides, canals, and underground cisterns to store water, and they turned the Negev into productive farmland. However, after AD 200, the irrigation works and terraces were destroyed and the Negev reverted to desert. In the twentieth century, Israeli farmers have again been reclaiming the Negev.

There are several ways to irrigate land. The most common is surface irrigation, whereby fields are either flooded or water is channelled through the furrows that separate the plants. Another technique is sprinkling. Rotating sprinklers can spray circular fields of more than 125 acres (50 hectares).

Surface irrigation is often carried out at night to reduce loss of water by evaporation. Trickle or drip irrigation, which was pioneered in Israel, reduces evaporation even more. It involves pumping water through thin plastic pipes containing holes. Water trickles through the holes, providing the correct amount of water for each plant in a row. Sheets of plastic around the plants reduce evaporation even further. Some pipes are placed underground so that the water goes directly to the roots.

Land reclamation and irrigation are costly to create and maintain. Care must be taken not to over-exploit the water in aquifers. There is another danger. Irrigation water can dissolve salts in the soil and if the land is not properly drained, the soil may become salty and useless for farming.

Mechanically controlled sprinklers, such as these in Israel, can enable large areas of desert to be reclaimed, when a suitable supply of water has been discovered.

Farming in deserts

The best known desert plant in the Old World is the date palm. Almost every part of the date palm is used. The dates are eaten or made into an alcoholic liquor, the trunk provides fuel and building material, the leaves are woven into mats and baskets, the fiber is used to make rope, and the pits can be ground into camel fodder or made into a coffee substitute.

Other oasis crops include cereals, citrus and other fruits, beans and vegetables. In the Negev Desert such luxury crops as apricots, avocados, and winter vegetables are grown in plastic covered greenhouses for export. Plants grown in these structures use only one-twentieth of the water needed in an open field.

Scientists are seeking new plants adapted to arid conditions. One desert plant that is now being grown commercially is the jojoba. It grows without

These giant grapefruit were grown in the Atacama Desert using water pumped from underground.

The date palm

Where deserts have been irrigated throughout North Africa and much of Asia the date palm can be found. It has also been introduced into the New World and Australia. The date palm has in the past brought great wealth to the oases of the Sahara, though it is not so important today. When the fruit is dried half its weight is sugar. This makes it a valuable food. A handful of dates can make a meal. They are eaten fresh, dried, or cooked in many different ways. The date palm is also important because every part of the palm can be used.

From the leaves mats and baskets can be woven

From the ribs of the fronds furniture can be made

The trunk can be used in housebuilding

The fruit can be eaten and it can be used in making alcohol, vinegar, and syrup

Rope can be made from the fruit stalks

This plastic tunnel is used for growing vegetables in the desert in Israel. It prevents water loss from evaporation.

irrigation in areas with no more than 3 in (80 mm) of rain a year. Its seeds yield an oil very similar to sperm whale oil which has many uses, including as an industrial lubricant.

Another plant, the guayale, grows wild only in the Chihuahuan Desert of north-central Mexico and southwestern Texas. It can be used to produce rubber. And triticale, a new hybrid of rye and wheat which makes excellent bread, is drought-resistant and tolerates salty soil. The chief producers are the Soviet Union and the United States.

Improved and new animal breeds are also being investigated. The saiga antelope in the deserts of the Soviet Union is being reared for its meat and leather. And the Israelis have produced a hybrid animal, the ya-ez, from the hardy Sinai goat, which can go for days without water, and the wild ibex, which yields tasty meat.

Terracing is an important means of conserving water for desert crops.

Mineral resources of deserts

Many desert regions contain valuable mineral resources. For instance, the desert nations of southwestern Asia play a leading role in the world trade in petroleum. Saudi Arabia is the world's chief oil-exporting country and the third largest producer, after the United States and the Soviet Union. Other major southwest Asian oil exporters are Iran, Iraq, Kuwait, the United Arab Emirates, and Bahrain. The Saharan nations of Libya, Algeria, and Tunisia are other oil exporters while Iran and Algeria are major producers of natural gas.

Oil has brought great wealth to some of the desert nations. Much of the money that comes from oil exports is used to finance social and welfare services, irrigation projects, and desalination plants to produce fresh water from sea water. Yet in most of these countries, there are still enormous differences between the standards of living of the rich and poor.

Some deserts contain minerals called evaporites. These were formed when lakes or arms of the sea dried up. Evaporites include gypsum, which is used to make plaster of Paris, and halite, or rock salt. The Atacama Desert in Chile also has huge deposits of sodium nitrate, which is used to make fertilizers. The importance of these reserves has declined now, because many fertilizers are made synthetically.

The deserts of the Soviet Union contain copper, gold, and oil, while the southwestern United States has deposits of valuable minerals such as, gold, silver, and uranium. The Australian Desert is one of the richest, with reserves of gold, iron ore, opals, and uranium.

Mining, however, presents many problems. Food, water, and other supplies often have to be brought in and the miners must be highly paid because, otherwise, they would not endure such unpleasant conditions.

Burning natural gas at an oilfield in Libya.
Oil and natural gas are often found together and are important resources of many North African countries.

Salt is an important resource of deserts. It may either be mined or the hot desert sun may be used to evaporate seawater from shallow pans leaving the salt behind.

The finest opals are found under the Australian deserts. The miners at places such as Coober Pedy both work and live underground because it is so hot.

Desertification

Deserts are on the march in some places because of human misuse of the land. Desertification, as scientists call it, is threatening more than a fifth of the earth's land area. It affects more than 100 countries.

South of the Sahara, a region called the Sahel has an average annual rainfall of 4–16 in (100–400 mm). In good years, there is pasture for the livestock of nomadic farmers and the far south has crop farms. In the early 1960s, the rainfall was abundant and the area of pasture increased, as also did the size of the herds. But severe droughts in the 1970s caused great destruction. The overly large herds devoured the dwindling plants and large areas were laid bare. Millions of animals died and their owners starved. The Sahara advanced southward by 328 ft (100 m) a year in places.

Three major causes of desertification are overgrazing, overcultivation, and the destruction of plant life. These factors are partly the result of a recent rapid increase in the human populations of desert lands – a consequence of better health services and higher standards of living.

Overgrazing, overcultivation, and deforestation expose the fragile soil to the wind. Without plant roots to bind it together, the dry soil breaks down into dust which is blown away by strong winds. In the 1930s, overcultivation turned the semi-arid Great Plains into a bleak "dust bowl." Millions of tons of fertile soil were lost.

Desertification also results from bad irrigation methods that waterlog the soil or make it salty. Insect pests, such as locusts, and introduced animals play a part. For example, rabbits introduced into Australia reduced the plant cover over large areas. Before their numbers were reduced by the disease myxomatosis, desertification had begun.

Rainstorms can wash away the soil where the plant cover has been removed by, for example, overgrazing.

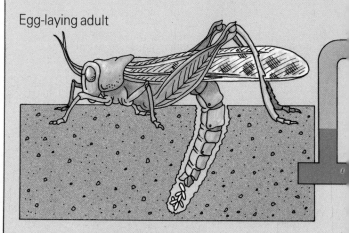

Locusts

Locusts are a type of grasshopper that periodically appear in great swarms. These swarms play a part in the spread of deserts by eating all the plants in their path. The swarms can travel great distances and cover vast areas.

Egg-laying adult

When an area has lost its plant cover duststorms can carry away the topsoil and leave a desert behind.

Gregarious or solitary?

The locust has two forms or phases. The solitary form lives alone and is widely scattered. After rain, when plants are abundant, the locust population increases rapidly. Then, as the ground dries and plants die, as food becomes scarce and the locusts become more crowded, the gregarious form becomes more common. The gregarious form likes to live in large groups, has larger wings, shorter legs, and is more active and nervous than the solitary form. Great swarms of the gregarious form take flight on warm dry days.

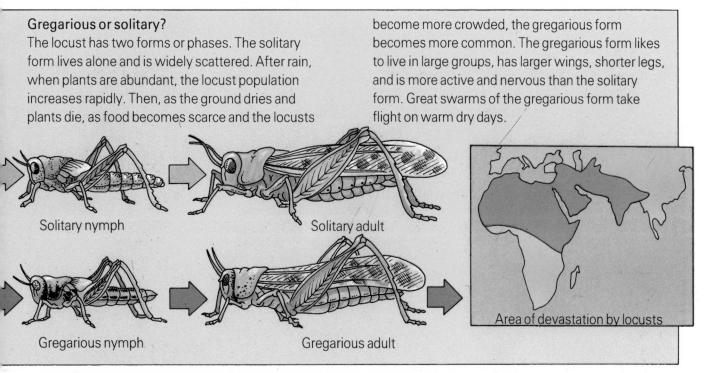

Solitary nymph

Solitary adult

Gregarious nymph

Gregarious adult

Area of devastation by locusts

Conservation in deserts

Experts estimate that over 15,000,000 acres (6,000,000 hectares) of useful land is being lost every year through desertification. What can be done to halt this destruction?

In the United States, millions of dollars were spent to stop wind erosion in the "dust bowl." Many farmers now rotate their crops so as to avoid overcultivation. They plant fallow land with such crops as clover, which protects the soil and, when plowed in, fertilizes the soil. Slopes are terraced or plowed along the contour to reduce water erosion during occasional downpours. Trees are planted to form wind breaks while various plants are used to anchor drifting soil. Because of this action, recent droughts have caused much less damage than those in the 1930s.

Better farming methods are also being applied elsewhere. In Ethiopia, where desertification caused starvation and death in the 1980s, farmer

The Arabian oryx has been saved from extinction by being bred in zoos before being re-released into the Arabian Desert.

These people in Somalia are planting brushwood to stabilize dunes. Though apparently dead, the brushwood will take root and sprout when the rains come.

This man is building crescents of stone to slow the run-off of water when it rains. More water will then soak into the soil and be available for plant growth.

associations have been founded. Members help to build terraces and dams to conserve water. They are also planting trees to protect the land, to provide food for animals, and to produce firewood.

In oil-rich countries, oil residues are sprayed on drifting sand. This binds the soil, allowing time for grasses, acacia, and eucalyptus to take root. As these plants grow, they create humus (rotted plant and animal remains). Humus is important, because it absorbs and retains moisture when rain occurs. Scientists have suggested that "green belts" around deserts could be created in this way.

Scientists are also studying major aquifers, some of which underlie several countries, to try to prevent their overuse. Satellites are providing information about the spread of deserts and also show where rain has recently fallen. This information can be used to exploit the resources of the desert more efficiently.

These trees have been planted in Abu Dhabi to restore fertility to the soil. The trees have been planted in hollows to make best use of available water. As they grow, the trees make humus.

Changing ways of life

In most desert lands, the ways of life of people are changing rapidly. In wealthy countries, with valuable resources, such as oil, more people are finding jobs in cities and towns. Hospitals, schools, and modern housing are making life more comfortable, while projects to develop the economy are being financed. For example, the cultivation of crops was once relatively unimportant in Saudi Arabia. But, mainly because of investment in costly irrigation projects, the area of cultivated land increased from 370,000 acres (150,000 hectares) in the mid-1970s to 4,900,000 acres (2,000,000 hectares) in 1986.

Prospects are bleak, however, for many people in poor desert countries that cannot finance, without massive foreign aid, the costly measures needed to combat desertification. The problem is made worse in many countries because of the fast rates of population growth. Overpopulation stretches the countries' resources. For example, the populations of the Sahelian nations (those in the Sahara Desert) are doubling every twenty-five to thirty years. By comparison, the population of Europe, excluding the Soviet Union, would take more than 170 years to double at current rates.

However, deserts have one great resource – sunshine – that has been barely exploited. Sunshine can be used to produce electrical energy. The sun generates 20,000 times more energy than is used at present. Some scientists think that large-scale solar power stations, using huge mirrors, could make desert countries the industrial centers of the future. And, with abundant cheap energy, the desalination of sea water, which is now expensive, would become feasible outside the oil-rich nations.

Given air-conditioned hotels, sunny deserts can attract tourists, as shown by the popularity of Palm Springs in California, seaside resorts in the Sinai Peninsula, and many scenic national parks in arid lands around the world.

For some desert dwellers, oil has brought great prosperity.

Hunter-gatherer groups of the desert, such as these Australian Aborigines, have often been forced to leave their traditional lands and end their nomadic lifestyle to live in shanty towns.

Glossary

Aquifer A layer of rock that absorbs water and allows it to flow slowly through.

Arthropods Small animals that have a hard covering or exoskeleton and jointed limbs but no backbone. Insects and spiders are arthropods.

Deforestation Extensive cutting of trees for timber or firewood. This can result in desertification.

Desalination The removal of salt from water. Several techniques are used, but all are expensive.

Desertification The expansion of deserts into areas that previously had more vegetation. This is usually due to overgrazing, overcultivation, and deforestation.

Doldrums A zone of low air pressure around the equator, where the sun's heat makes the air rise.

Drought A lengthy period without any significant precipitation. Droughts may continue for many years in deserts.

Dust bowl A dry region in which the wind has removed much of the topsoil. Dust bowls are caused by overcultivation.

Ephemeral A word meaning short-lived, it is also applied to plants that have a life cycle of six to eight weeks. Their seeds may lie dormant for many years.

Fallow land Land left without crops for some time.

Fault A place where the rocks of the Earth's crust have broken and moved. This happens due to the forces within the Earth that produce earthquakes. During an earthquake a fault may occur.

Gregarious Animals that live together in groups.

Ground water Water that is found within the rocks underlying land areas. It accounts for about 0.625 percent of the world's total water supply.

Horse latitudes Zones of permanent high air pressure around latitudes 30° north and 30° south.

Hybrid An offspring of parents of different varieties or species. It is applied mainly to plants, including food crops, and also to some animals.

Latitude The distance of a place north or south of the equator measured in degrees.

Leeward The side, for example of a mountain range, sheltered from the wind.

Myxomatosis A South American rabbit disease that was introduced into a number of countries to reduce the numbers of wild rabbits.

Nomads People who move from place to place, often in search of food or for plants on which their herds can graze.

Ocean currents Relatively fast-moving flows of water in the oceans. They may be cold or warm, according to whether they originated around the poles or in the tropics.

Old World Before Columbus sailed to the Americas the world for Europeans consisted of Europe, Africa, and Asia. This is what is known as the Old World.

Sahelian nations Countries that have their boundaries within the Sahara Desert.

Soil erosion The removal of topsoil resulting from human misuse of the land. Natural erosion occurs at a far slower rate.

Subtropics The regions that lie between the tropics and the temperate regions. Their climate is warmer than that of the temperate regions and, unlike the tropics, they are not wet all year round.

Terracing The building of level, step-like fields down hillsides to reduce soil erosion.

Windward The side, for example of a mountain range, that faces the wind.

Left Buttes in Monument Valley, Arizona.

Further Reading

Carson, James, *Deserts and People* (Silver Burdett Press, 1982) (1).

Cuisin, Michael, *Desert Dwellers* (Silver Burdett Press, 1987).

Dixon, Dougal, *Deserts and Wastelands* (Franklin Watts, 1985).

George, Uwe, *In the Deserts of this Earth* (Harcourt Brace Jovanovich, Inc. 1979).

Luling, Virginia, *Aborigines* (Silver Burdett Press, 1987).

National Geographic Society *A Look at the Earth Around Us: Deserts* (National Geographic Society, 1981).

Page, Jake, *Arid Lands* (Time-Life Books, 1984).

Peters, Stella, *Bedouins* (Silver Burdett Press, 1980).

Rochegaude, Anne, *My Village in the Sahara: Tarlift, Tuareg Boy* (Silver Burdett Press, 1985).

Sanders, John, *All About Deserts* (Troll Associates, 1984).

Van der Post, Laurens, *Lost World of the Kalahari* (Harcourt Brace Jovanovich, Inc. 1977).

Wagner, Fredrick H., *Wildlife of the Deserts* (Harry N. Abrams, 1981).

Picture acknowledgments

The publishers would like to thank the following for allowing their photographs to be reproduced in this book: Bruce Coleman Limited front cover (main picture/M.P.L. Fogden) (inset/C.B. Frith), 8 (Michael Freeman), 17 (Gerald Cubitt), 19 (top/Carol Hughes), 20 (David Hughes), 21 (both/David Hughes), 22 (top/Jen and Des Bartlett), 23 (top/Stephen J. Krasemann) (bottom/Carol Hughes), 40 (top/World Wildlife Fund and H. Jungius); GeoScience Features Library 9, 15 (top), 19 (bottom), 24 (top), 29; Hutchison Library 27 (inset), 30, 36 (right), 41 (bottom); Andrew Kelly 44; Oxfam (Jeremy Hartley) 38, 39, 40 (bottom), 41 (top); Wayland Picture Library, back cover, 15 (bottom), 25 (right), 34, 35 (bottom), 42–3 (both); ZEFA 6 (V. Englebert), 7 (Dr Biedermann), 11 (inset/J. Bitsch) (main picture/K. Scholz), 12 (Robin Smith), 13 (Günter Heil), 22 (bottom/A.P.L.), 24 (bottom/W. Backhaus), 26–7 (main picture/R. Smith), 31 (Foto Leidmann), 32–3, 35 (top/Bill Holden), 36 (left/Ziesmann), 37 (A.P.L.). All artwork is by Nick May.

Index